The Great Depression and World War II

(1929-1945)

★★ PRESIDENTS OF THE UNITED STATES ★★

By Marty Gitlin

WEIGL PUBLISHERS INC.

Published by Weigl Publishers Inc.
350 5th Avenue, Suite 3304 PMB 6G
New York, NY 10118-0069
Website: www.weigl.com

Library of Congress Cataloging-in-Publication Data

Gitlin, Marty.
  The Great Depression and World War II / Marty Gitlin.
      p. cm. -- (Presidents of the United States)
  Includes bibliographical references and index.
  ISBN 978-1-59036-749-0 (hard cover : alk. paper) -- ISBN 978-1-59036-750-6 (soft cover : alk. paper)
  1. Presidents--United States--Biography--Juvenile literature. 2. Presidents--United States--History--20th century--Juvenile literature. 3. United States--History--1933-1945--Juvenile literature. 4. United States--Politics and government--1933-1945--Juvenile literature. 5. Depressions--1929--United States--Juvenile literature. 6. World War, 1939-1945--United States--Juvenile literature. I. Title.
  E176.1.G578 2008
  973.09'9--dc22
  [B]
                                    2007012648

Printed in the United States of America
1 2 3 4 5 6 7 8 9 0 11 10 09 08 07

Project Coordinator
Heather C. Hudak

Design
Terry Paulhus

Photo Credits
Every reasonable effort has been made to trace ownership and to obtain permission to reprint copyright material. The publishers would be pleased to have any errors or omissions brought to their attention so that they may be corrected in subsequent printings.

All of the Internet URLs given in the book were valid at the time of publication. However, due to the dynamic nature of the Internet, some addresses may have changed, or sites may have ceased to exist since publication. While the author and publisher regret any inconvenience this may cause readers, no responsibility for any such changes can be accepted by either the author or the publisher.

Contents

United States Presidents

REVOLUTION AND THE NEW NATION (1750–EARLY 1800s)

 George Washington
(1789–1797)

 John Adams
(1797–1801)

 Thomas Jefferson
(1801–1809)

 James Madison
(1809–1817)

 James Monroe
(1817–1825)

EXPANSION AND REFORM (EARLY 1800s–1861)

 John Quincy Adams
(1825–1829)

 Andrew Jackson
(1829–1837)

 Martin Van Buren
(1837–1841)

 William Henry Harrison
(1841)

 John Tyler
(1841–1845)

 James Polk
(1845–1849)

 Zachary Taylor
(1849–1850)

 Millard Fillmore
(1850–1853)

 Franklin Pierce
(1853–1857)

 James Buchanan
(1857–1861)

CIVIL WAR AND RECONSTRUCTION (1850–1877)

 Abraham Lincoln
(1861–1865)

 Andrew Johnson
(1865–1869)

 Ulysses S. Grant
(1869–1877)

DEVELOPMENT OF THE INDUSTRIAL UNITED STATES (1870–1900)

 Rutherford B. Hayes
(1877–1881)

 James Garfield
(1881)

 Chester Arthur
(1881–1885)

 Grover Cleveland
(1885–1889)
(1893–1897)

 Benjamin Harrison
(1889–1893)

 William McKinley
(1897–1901)

THE EMERGENCE OF MODERN AMERICA (1890–1930)

 Theodore Roosevelt
(1901–1909)

 William H. Taft
(1909–1913)

 Woodrow Wilson
(1913–1921)

 Warren Harding
(1921–1923)

 Calvin Coolidge
(1923–1929)

THE GREAT DEPRESSION AND WORLD WAR II (1929–1945)

 Herbert Hoover
(1929–1933)

 Franklin D. Roosevelt
(1933–1945)

POST-WAR UNITED STATES (1945–EARLY 1970s)

 Harry S. Truman
(1945–1953)

 Dwight Eisenhower
(1953–1961)

 John F. Kennedy
(1961–1963)

 Lyndon Johnson
(1963–1969)

CONTEMPORARY UNITED STATES (1968 TO THE PRESENT)

 Richard Nixon
(1969–1974)

 Gerald Ford
(1974–1977)

 Jimmy Carter
(1977–1981)

 Ronald Reagan
(1981–1989)

 George H. W. Bush
(1989–1993)

 William J. Clinton
(1993–2001)

George W. Bush
(2001–)

The Great Depression and World War II

"Together we cannot fail."
Franklin D. Roosevelt to the American people in concluding his "Fireside Chat" speeches on the radio

Franklin D. Roosevelt led the United States through the Great Depression and World War II.

The 1920s was a prosperous and carefree period in American history. The role of the United States in achieving victory in World War I had given Americans a feeling of invincibility. That triumph, and the millions of immigrants seeking a better life in America, helped make the country a beacon of freedom in the minds and hearts of its citizens.

The economy was strong, and most people were enjoying their lives. On October 29, 1929, a **stock market** crash set off an economic crisis the scope of which America had never experienced. The Great **Depression** that extended through the 1930s not only wreaked havoc in this country, but spilled over into Europe. It played a role in future events that would lead to World War II.

Newly elected President Herbert Hoover had no political experience. His efforts to control the disaster failed. A lack of spending caused businesses to close and to lay off employees. Unemployment spread across the nation. The Great Depression frustrated Hoover's efforts to improve the economy. As a result, voters elected Franklin D. Roosevelt into office in 1932. He instituted a massive public works program, giving millions of people jobs on government-funded projects. He dubbed his policy "The New Deal."

Meanwhile, war was brewing in Europe. The depression had been particularly hard on Germany, which was still reeling from its defeat in World War I and was struggling to pay its war debts. The mark, which is the German currency, became virtually worthless. **Nazi** leader Adolf Hitler took advantage of the people's misery and promised them a better life. He was appointed Chancellor of Germany and quickly eliminated all political opposition to his rule. Hitler then prepared for war.

Germany began World War II by invading Poland in 1939. The invasion provoked England and France to declare war. The United States was officially neutral, but Roosevelt was clear in his opposition to the **Axis Powers** of Germany, Japan, and Italy. These three countries had formed an alliance to expand their power throughout the rest of the world. The American economy was boosted by the production of war materials to help the **Allies**, the countries opposed to the Axis Powers.

The United States entered the war on December 7, 1941, when the Japanese bombed naval bases at Pearl Harbor in Hawai'i. The American effort proved a critical turning point in the war. U.S. forces helped defeat Germany, which had conquered much of Europe, and Japan, which had conquered much of Asia.

In 1945, the United States ushered in the nuclear age. To end the war with Japan, atomic bombs were dropped on the Japanese cities of Hiroshima and Nagasaki. The frightening capacity for destruction of nuclear bombs would forever change the world. Humans were now capable of destroying the world. The responsibility of its leaders to prevent that from happening was enormous.

Herbert Hoover's Early Years

It has been said that America is the land of opportunity, a country in which a person from the humblest beginnings can become president. No stronger case for that argument can be made than Herbert Hoover.

Hoover was born on August 10, 1874, in the small farming town of West Branch, Iowa. His father was a blacksmith, who also earned money selling plows, wagons, and barbed wire. His mother raised him and his brother, Tad, and his sister, May. Hoover grew up with a strong work ethic. His parents taught him about the importance of money by paying him to do chores. Among those duties was picking potato bugs, for which he received one penny for every 100 bugs.

> **"Fishing is much more than fish. It is the great occasion when we may return to the fine simplicity of our forefathers."**
>
> *Herbert Hoover, on one of his favorite childhood activities*

Hoover's family was devoutly Quaker. They attended religious services at the Quaker meetinghouse every Sunday. Hoover's mother often spoke during these gatherings, but much of the morning was spent in quiet contemplation of the Quaker belief that one must feel the presence of God. Quakers also have a strong belief against participating in wars.

The unexpected deaths of his father to heart trouble and his mother to pneumonia made orphans of Hoover and his siblings. Hoover was only 9 years old. He had always been a shy boy, but the loss of his parents played a role in making his shyness a permanent trait.

Herbert Hoover grew up to be a mining engineer and the 31st president of the United States.

Hoover moved to live with his uncle, Dr. Henry John Minthorn, in Oregon. A strict man and a determined worker, Minthorn instilled in his nephew a strong sense of responsibility. Hoover was kept busy tending horses and cutting down fir trees. He left high school to work at his uncle's real estate office for $30 a month.

In 1891, Hoover befriended Robert Brown, an engineer who had stopped by. Hoover was an average student in most subjects, but he excelled in math. Brown helped him develop an interest in engineering. Hoover's parents and his uncle had planned for him to attend a Quaker college, and his uncle was disappointed when he enrolled at a new California school, Stanford University.

A pronounced shyness in new social situations made college life difficult for Hoover. He made few friends at Stanford, so he immersed himself in his studies. He developed a fascination with geology, the study of the physical history of Earth and the rocks that it is composed of. He geared himself toward a career as a mining engineer. At Stanford, Hoover met Lou Henry. She was the only woman in the geology department.

Hoover graduated from Stanford in 1895 with a geology degree and $40 in his pocket. At first, he struggled to find a good job. Out of college, he worked in a gold mine, pushing ore carts 70 hours a week and earning up to 25 cents an hour.

Herbert Hoover was born in a small farm house in West Branch, Iowa.

Hoover's Rise to the Presidency

Herbert Hoover received his first professional break when he landed a typist job with western mining expert Louis Janin. Hoover was appointed to managing positions in New Mexico and Colorado. In the fall of 1896, Janin recommended him for work with the British firm of Bewick, Moreing and Company. Hoover was hired to survey and evaluate gold mines in Australia. He rose quickly in the company. Hoover was offered an opportunity to manage mines in China.

"A Chicken in Every Pot, Two Cars in Every Garage."
Herbert Hoover's election promise in 1928

During this time, Hoover felt that he was making enough money to get married. He and Lou Henry were wed February 10, 1899. They would have two sons, Herbert, Jr., and Allan. Both would have careers in engineering, like their father. In China, Hoover became entangled in the Boxer Rebellion. A group of Chinese nationalists set out to destroy every Western and Christian influence in China. They feared people from other countries would exploit China's wealth and ruin its culture. In Tianjin, China, Hoover directed the building of barricades and the provision of food to the foreign community who lived there, until the arrival of relief forces. The rebellion ended in 1901.

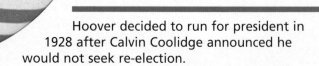

Hoover decided to run for president in 1928 after Calvin Coolidge announced he would not seek re-election.

When Hoover left China, he became part owner of Bewick, Moreing and Company, and traveled the globe. He started his own business and worked with countries all over the world, such as Russia. The more he worked with foreign governments, the more he believed in the United States' democratic system.

Hoover developed a strong sense of community and a firm commitment to helping people because of his Quaker upbringing. In 1914, as World War I was gearing up, Hoover headed the America Relief Committee. This group helped thousands of Americans who were stranded in Europe during the war. He worked as director of the Commission for the Relief of Belgium and the American Relief Administration. In these positions, he helped distribute billions of dollars of food, clothing, and other supplies to people in need.

Hoover's efforts earned him national and worldwide recognition. In 1917, President Woodrow Wilson asked Hoover to serve as Food Administrator after the United States entered World War I. He oversaw food production by farmers, the allotment of food to U.S. troops overseas, and the prices of food sold at grocery stores. Some people complained that the position gave Hoover too much power. However, his work helped conserve food and feed American forces and their European allies, who won the war in 1918. That same year, Hoover served as an economic advisor to President Woodrow Wilson.

In 1921, Republican President Warren Harding appointed Hoover to be secretary of commerce. In this position, he oversaw the growth of U.S. businesses and industries. Hoover served as secretary of commerce through Republican Calvin Coolidge's presidency.

Before the 1928 presidential election, Coolidge announced that he would not run for re-election. Hoover decided to enter the race, even though he had never run for political office before. Hoover easily won the Republican Party nomination. He went on to beat Democrat Alfred E. Smith in the election by more than six million votes, one of the largest margins of victory in U.S. history.

Herbert Hoover (right) oversaw the shipping of supplies from the United States to war-ravaged Europe.

Hoover's Quest for Peace

Though economic troubles would force Hoover to focus on domestic affairs, he also concerned himself with several foreign policy problems. Hoover was greatly affected by the ravages of World War I. Millions died. Many people called it "the war to end all wars" because they did not think the world could afford a war of similar scope. Even though Hoover had become a multi-millionaire, he gave up his business during the war to help others. This earned him the nickname "The Great Humanitarian." Hoover embraced Quaker beliefs against armed conflict. Like many world leaders in the years following World War I, Hoover's primary objective was to develop friendships with other nations to avoid more bloodshed.

> **"Older men declare war. But it is the youth that must fight and die."**
> *Herbert Hoover, on keeping the peace after World War I*

Between the 1928 election and his 1929 inauguration, Hoover traveled throughout Latin America. He announced his friendly intentions to the governments in this part of the world, including countries past presidents had disapproved of. When he took office, he immediately withdrew U.S. forces from Nicaragua. Some Latin American nations refused to pay debts owed to the United States or took anti-American stands. Hoover, however, treated them all with respect. His friendly policy helped improve relations in the region.

Europe and Asia were another matter. While the United States and most of Europe worked to maintain peace, people seeking power in Germany, and those who had already gained control in Japan and Italy, were taking a more aggressive approach.

Japanese troops marched into Manchuria, China, occupying the region during the 1930s.

Adolf Hitler, chancellor of Germany and leader of the Nazi Party, was welcomed by his supporters in Nuremberg.

In 1931, Japan's army seized control of the government. Shortly afterward, Japan invaded Manchuria, which is the northeastern part of China. Hoover did not approve of Japan's actions, but he was against the idea of U.S. involvement. He knew the U.S. military was ill-prepared for a war in Asia and that most Americans would not favor a war in such a far off place. Hoover refused to apply economic sanctions against Japan.

Hoover took a similar approach when fascist regimes took control in Italy and Spain. These strict dictatorships believed in stripping their citizens of their liberties for the good of the nation. Hoover did nothing when the Nazi Party took control of Germany. Nazism was similar to fascism, but it also stressed the purity of the German people.

With the increasing power of these governments, some countries called for the creation of an international army to act as a world keeper of the peace.

Hoover opposed the idea. Instead, he called for all nations to reduce their military forces. He believed a war could be avoided through dialogue rather than a show of force.

THE STIMSON DOCTRINE

The League of Nations was formed following World War I. The goal of this international organization was to prevent wars and solve conflicts between nations.

When Japan invaded Manchuria, Secretary of State Henry Stimson declared that the U.S. government would not recognize Japan's rights to territory it had seized in China. The League of Nations adopted Stimson's policy, which became known as The Stimson Doctrine. However, it proved ineffective. Japan simply withdrew from the League of Nations and completed its takeover of Manchuria.

Hoover's Presidency

Between the election and his inauguration, Hoover warned that there might come a time when he would suffer because the American people would ask him to solve a problem that could not be easily solved. Hoover had no idea how true this statement would be.

When Hoover took office in 1929, he set out to better the lives of America's underprivileged. He asked for conferences on housing and child health. He organized groups to look into improving education and law enforcement. Hoover worked on prison reform and worked to improve health care for American Indians.

Hoover strongly supported farmers. He helped pass the Agricultural Marketing Act, which gave farmers more freedom to sell their own crops. This law established the Federal Farm Board, an organization created to stabilize the price of farm goods and assure farmers a fair price for their crops.

"I'm the only person of distinction who has ever had a depression named after him."

Herbert Hoover, on continuing criticism of his attempts to end the economic crisis

The American public applauded Hoover's efforts. The economy was doing well in the 1920s, and people did not mind sharing in the success. By the end of the decade, events collapsed on Hoover's ideas. The stock market crashed in 1929. Billions of dollars were lost. The country was on the verge of its largest economic disaster, and people looked to Hoover for help. He and his

Herbert Hoover delivered his inaugural speech to the nation on March 4, 1929.

People often waited in "bread lines" for food during the Great Depression.

advisors, however, did not realize how serious the problem was until millions of people were unemployed.

As Food Administrator, Hoover had been given free reign to take whatever measures he deemed appropriate in the time of war. As president, his suggestions had to be accepted by **Congress**. Hoover's fellow Republicans could not agree on a solution to the economic problems. Secretary of the Treasury Andrew Mellon simply stated that economic problems would force people to work harder. Democrats did not mind voters being angry at Hoover. They knew there was another election in a few years, and the Democratic candidate would win if Hoover lost public support. As a result, the financial crisis worsened as Hoover's hands were tied and Congress argued over what to do.

PROHIBITION

Prohibition began in 1920, when the 18th Amendment took effect. This amendment outlawed the manufacture, transportation, and sale of alcoholic beverages.

Hoover supported stronger law enforcement, and he was worried about the growing crime rate surrounding prohibition. He established the Wickersham Commission, named after former Attorney General George W. Wickersham, to investigate. The commission's investigation revealed that enforcement of prohibition had failed. Despite the law, people continued to make and sell alcohol.

In 1933, the 21st Amendment was enacted into law. It repealed the 18th Amendment, lifting the restrictions on the manufacture, transportation, and sale of alcoholic beverages.

The Great Depression

"No one in his place could have done more. Very few of his predecessors could have done as much." New York Times *article in the spring of 1930 on Hoover's role in the Stock Market Crash*

The "Roaring 20s" was a cheerful time in America. Most people enjoyed a carefree lifestyle resulting from a strong economy. Many people wanted to further their wealth. They began investing in the stock market, purchasing shares of businesses. Some people started buying and selling stocks quickly to earn fast cash. This practice was called speculation. Banks began speculating, but they did so with their customers' money.

The stock market showed signs of weakening in October of 1929. Many investors began selling their stocks. Stock prices rise when stocks are bought and fall as they are sold. On October 24, 1929, also known as Black Thursday, stock prices began to tumble as a sell off began. A few days later, on the 29th, the stock market crashed. President Herbert Hoover had been in office for just less than eight months.

The Great Depression was the worst economic period in U.S. history. Investors and banks lost billions of dollars in a single day. Banks closed, and people lost their life savings. Afterward, most people could only afford the basic necessities, food, clothes, and medicine. Many others could not even afford these items.

People did not have much money to spend, so they bought fewer goods. Many businesses had to close or fire employees because no one was buying

People on Wall Street in New York City anxiously awaited news during the financial crash on "Black Tuesday."

The Great Depression left many families homeless. Roadside camps made of lean-tos sprung up all over the United States.

their products. This meant that fewer people had jobs or money to spend, which led to more businesses closing. The number of Americans out of work rose to 5 million in 1930 and to 8 million in 1931.

The confidence that Americans had gained throughout the 1920s was shattered. They looked to Hoover to save the country. They believed his work as Food Administrator could be useful in fixing the economy. Many wondered if Hoover, who had little political experience, would be able to find a solution. Their worst fear was that the problem was too big for any one person to fix quickly.

RECONSTRUCTION FINANCE CORPORATION

Hoover believed that if banks continued to fail, the U.S. economy would also fail. So in 1932, he persuaded Congress to create the Reconstruction Finance Corporation (RFC), which was designed to help the banking industry. The RFC loaned banks over $2 billion. It also gave money to state and local governments and various businesses.

Hoover felt that this money would trickle down throughout the economy and give people more money to spend, thereby helping businesses. Some of the money was never dispersed, and much of it was used for political purposes. The RFC continued for more than a decade, but its impact was too little to stem the tide of the Great Depression.

Hoover's Response to the Great Depression

Hoover made many attempts to help the economy. He signed the Hawley-Smoot Tariff in 1930. This law raised taxes on imported goods. Hoover hoped it would protect businesses from foreign competition. However, the law began a global tariff war in which other countries also raised taxes on imported goods. Instead of helping businesses at home, the law hurt the businesses by making it more difficult to trade goods overseas.

Even when Hoover managed to have success with his policies, those very policies seemed to fail. The Federal Farm Board, which Hoover created to help farmers, purchased 257 million bushels of wheat from farmers. But the Federal Farm Board could not find anyone to buy the crops, which resulted in a loss of $345 million. Then in 1930, a drought worsened things for farmers as their crops began to fail.

Hoover convinced businesses not to cut wages, so workers would have enough money to spend. He hoped this would spur the economy. Disallowing wage cuts, however, gave some businesses no other choice but to lay off employees. Instead of having less money to spend, fired workers had no money to spend. As the Great Depression worsened, large companies, such as U.S. Steel and Ford Motor Company, began cutting wages again in 1931. Other businesses soon followed.

Herbert Hoover's attempts to help struggling farmers failed, and many protested his inability to relieve their suffering.

Hoover feared that giving money directly to those in need would make them dependent on the government. He believed the government should help people help themselves. The Great Depression had taken the spirit out of many Americans. With no jobs available, they did not know of any ways to help themselves. They had enough to worry about simply finding food, clothing, and shelter.

Hoover established some programs that helped people. The Relief and Reconstriction Act was the first unemployment assistance program. It created jobs through public works programs, such as building docks and railroads. The Federal Home Loan Bank Act was passed to help lower the cost of home ownership. The President's Organization for Unemployment Relief was established to help the millions who had lost their jobs during the Great Depression. Hoover, however, angered the struggling American people by asking

Some people who lost their homes were forced to live in shacks. These rows of shacks were called "Hoovervilles" or "shanty towns."

Congress to raise taxes in 1932, so the federal government would not go into debt.

By 1933, 25 percent of the nation's work force was unemployed. Homeless people could be seen everywhere. Millions stood in lines at soup kitchens just to be fed. The homeless built rows of shacks, which people called "Hoovervilles" as a reference to the president they felt had failed them. Newspapers came to be called "Hoover blankets." Some people turned their pockets inside out to show they had no money, calling this practice "waving Hoover flags."

> **"I am confident that our people have the resources to meet this situation in the way they have met their problems over generations."**
> *Herbert Hoover, on the role of Americans in trying to overcome the Great Depression*

The Bonus Army Crisis

I n 1924, Congress had voted to give a "bonus" to the people who had served during World War I. It was an easy promise to make at the time. The economy was healthy, and Americans were grateful to the soldiers who had helped win the war. War World I **veterans** would receive $1.25 for every day they served overseas and $1 for every day they served in the United States. The bonus would not be paid out until 1945.

In 1932, however, the veterans decided they could not wait to receive their payments. Nearly 15,000 veterans and their family members marched to Washington, D.C. They became known as the Bonus Army. They set up ramshackle camps near the Capitol as Congress voted on the Patman Bonus Bill, which would move forward the date of the bonus payout.

World War I veterans marched on the Capitol to demand early payment of the bonus the U.S. government had promised them.

The bill passed in the U.S. House of Representatives, but it was voted down in the Senate. After the defeat of the bill, Congress gave people money to return home. Some of the marchers accepted the funds and left, but many others continued to stay. Like many Americans, they had no money for food or other essentials. Their only hope was that the government would help them.

In July of that year, police tried to remove some of the remaining Bonus Army protesters. Two marchers were shot and killed. Protesters attacked the police, wounding some of them. The police then asked the president for help.

Hoover called in federal troops led by General Douglas MacArthur, who would later gain fame in World War II. Cavalry troops, led by Major George Patton and Major Dwight Eisenhower, gathered near the Capitol as thousands of people poured into the street to watch.

The marchers assumed the cavalry had arrived to protect them. Instead, they charged the veterans with bayonets, tanks, and gas bombs. Against Hoover's direct orders, the camp was burned to the ground. One 7-year-old boy was stabbed. An injured infant was rushed to the hospital and later died. Nearby hospitals were overcrowded with injured veterans.

The fiasco could not have come at a worse time for Hoover. The 1932 election was near at hand, and people began to criticize Hoover for being heartless and uncaring of people's suffering during the Great Depression.

"Shame, Shame!"

The screaming spectators who witnessed soldiers charging the Bonus Army marchers near the Capitol in Washington

World War I veterans camped outside the Capitol as they waited for the U.S. Senate to vote on the Patman Bonus Bill.

Hoover's Final Years in Government

Though television would later add to its importance in presidential **campaigns**, personality was already a major factor to voters in 1932. Herbert Hoover's reserved demeanor, dry speaking style, and grim expression did not woo the American people when he ran against Democrat Franklin D. Roosevelt. On the other hand, Roosevelt spoke with energy and an air of confidence.

Roosevelt's personality certainly played a large role in the election. More importantly, however, was that Hoover was being blamed for the worst economic period in the nation's history. Unemployment and homelessness were increasing as his term in office went on. The Bonus Army crisis only served to make Hoover appear less caring in the minds of the voters.

Radios were now in 12 million U.S. homes. During the 1932 campaign, both candidates gave more than 100 speeches, heard across the country. Voters were more informed about the candidates than ever before. Roosevelt, however, was a far more effective and persuasive speaker than Hoover.

Hoover gave the impression that he was asking the people to do more to overcome the Great Depression. Roosevelt, however, offered ways for the government to help businesses and the unemployed to get back on their feet. The election results were predictable. Hoover received the electoral votes from only six of the 48 states. Roosevelt garnered 23 million votes to just 16 million for Hoover. Hoover won in a landslide in 1928. He lost in a landslide in 1932.

Hoover hoped that Roosevelt would consult him about the economic crisis, but the new president never did. Hoover spoke out against Roosevelt's "New Deal" policies in a book called *The Challenge to Liberty* in 1934.

> **"Hoover will be known as the greatest innocent bystander in history…full of courage and patriotism, undaunted to the last…a brave man fighting valiantly, futilely to the end."**
>
> *Radio commentator on the defeated President Hoover after the 1932 election*

By this time, Hoover was so unpopular that Roosevelt changed the name of a huge dam being built on the Colorado River from Hoover Dam to Boulder Dam. Hoover was not invited to the dam's opening ceremonies in 1935, even though it was his work as secretary of commerce that initiated the project.

In 1936, the Republicans nominated Kansas Governor Alf Landon to run against Roosevelt. Landon asked that Hoover not make speeches in support of him. Hoover was shunned by his own party.

When the United States entered World War II, Hoover once again helped people in need. He headed relief organizations in Poland, Finland, and Belgium. Hoover continued to oppose U.S. involvement in wars. He was against the United States getting involved in World War II, until the attack on Pearl Harbor. Hoover was against dropping atomic bombs on Japan, and he did not support U.S. involvement in the Korean War.

Toward the end of his political career, Hoover befriended President Harry Truman. Truman appointed Hoover to be the chairman of the Commission on Organization of the Executive Branch of the Government in 1947. This position was formed to cut unneeded offices in the federal government. Hoover's efforts saved the government billions of dollars. Hoover helped establish the Department of Defense and the Department of Health, Education, and Welfare. Truman decided to rename the former president's project along the Colorado River "Hoover Dam," because of Hoover's service to the U.S. government.

After World War II ended, Herbert Hoover traveled to Europe to head up relief efforts in countries such as Poland.

Hoover's Legacy

Herbert Hoover could not foresee or control the troubles that would come during his presidency. Though Hoover warned Americans about speculative investing, which is the practice of buying and selling stocks quickly for profit, no one had an inkling of the looming economic disaster. When the stock market crash of 1929 put the Great Depression in motion, there were no previous events in U.S. history that Hoover could draw guidance from. Even the economic troubles of the Panic of 1837, during President Martin Van Buren's time, could not compare to the hardships faced throughout the Great Depression.

> **"He has worked hard; he has been very brave; he has endured."**
> *A Quaker friend during Hoover's eulogy in 1964*

One factor that weighed against Hoover was his quiet, respectful demeanor. Other presidents had strong oratory skills and charismatic personalities that could sway lawmakers to take action or make citizens agree with their views. Hoover did not possess these traits. What voters deemed positive traits in 1928 were seen four years later as weaknesses. The public sought an outspoken and confident leader when Franklin D. Roosevelt was elected.

Hoover had always preached self-sufficiency and the power of the individual to make the most out of his or her life. The Great Depression, however, brought with it a demand for government help. Many people believed Hoover thought they should work harder to get themselves and the country out of trouble. When it became apparent that the government needed to step in, people thought it was too little, too late. Many believed the Bonus Army crisis showed Hoover to be heartless and unwilling to help those in need.

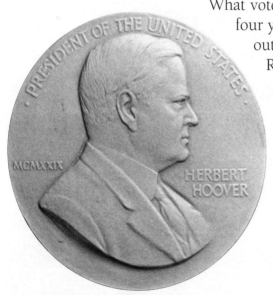

Coins and stamps have been created to honor Herbert Hoover for his service to the United States.

The Boulder Dam, renamed Hoover Dam, was completed in 1935.

However, Hoover is now remembered as a patriotic American who fought for what he believed was best for the country. His contributions as Food Administrator during World War I cannot be overlooked. Though many saw Hoover as an impersonal leader, his desire for peace tells a different story. Nobody has ever doubted the love Hoover had for his country and the work ethic he showed in trying to make it a better place to live.

At age 86, Hoover spoke at the 1960 Republican national convention. Four years later, Hoover developed a bleeding ulcer in his stomach. Hoover passed away on October 20, 1964, at age 90.

Herbert Hoover compiled many reports to help make the government run more efficiently.

Franklin D. Roosevelt's Early Years

Franklin Delano Roosevelt was born on January 30, 1882, to a wealthy family. His father, James, gained wealth in the railroad and coal industries. He had earned enough money to purchase an estate in Hyde Park, New York.

Young Roosevelt spent his childhood playing around his family's vast estate, which was surrounded by acres of fields, woods, and gardens. The environment of Hyde Park grew into a passion. Roosevelt developed a fondness for the country and for farming that would stay with him the rest of his life.

Roosevelt grew up in a home with a staff of servants.

Roosevelt was pampered growing up. A staff of servants attended to his every need at the estate. His parents provided all the love and material goods any child could ask for. They expanded Roosevelt's horizons by taking him to Europe. They traveled throughout New England and spent time at a family-owned cottage on Campobello Island in Canada.

Roosevelt's mother was protective of her son. She hired teachers to tutor Roosevelt at the estate rather than send him away to school. He remained home-schooled until the age of 14, when he entered Groton, a private boys school in Massachusetts. Later in life, Roosevelt would credit the school's headmaster, Reverend Dr. Endicott Peabody, for helping to shape his character. Peabody maintained strict discipline and nurtured loyalty to God and country.

Roosevelt and Eleanor had five children. They were Elliot, James, Franklin, Jr., John, and Anna.

Roosevelt's cousin, Theodore, then governor of New York, spoke at Franklin's high school graduation. Theodore would help influence Roosevelt to pursue a political career of his own. After high school, Roosevelt enrolled at Harvard University. He was an average student but excelled in several activities. He was a captain on the Newell Boating Club and became editor-in-chief of the college newspaper, the Crimson. Roosevelt continued his education at Columbia Law School but never graduated.

While attending Columbia, Roosevelt began to spend time with Theodore's niece, Eleanor. The pair were married in March 1905.

At the age of 25, Roosevelt began a career in law. Even though he had not graduated from law school, he passed the bar, an exam people must pass if they wish to practice law. His career in law would not last long, however. With Theodore already serving his second term as president, politics were in Roosevelt's future.

"More than 40 years ago you said something about not losing your boyhood ideals in later life. Those were Groton ideals—taught by you —and your words are still with."

Franklin D. Roosevelt, in a note he sent former teacher Endicott Peabody in 1941

Roosevelt's Rise to Politics

In 1910, Roosevelt's reassuring style and ability to persuade others helped him win a seat in the New York state senate. He traveled more than 2,000 miles throughout his district, taking his ideas to the people. He would have his touring car halted on a whim, so he could get out to chat with people. Roosevelt ran as a Democrat, even though his cousin, Theodore, was a Republican.

During his time in office, Roosevelt came across as being honest, which was a reputation he maintained for the rest of his career. He vowed to fight against dishonesty wherever he could find it. Roosevelt backed organized labor, whose battle for shorter work weeks and more pay often met with violent reactions from employers. Roosevelt supported the campaign for women's right to vote. Roosevelt easily won a second term.

In 1912, Roosevelt gave his support to Woodrow Wilson as the Democratic **nominee** for president. After Wilson was elected president, he rewarded Roosevelt by making him

Franklin D. Roosevelt vigorously campaigned for political office.

assistant secretary of the navy. Roosevelt enjoyed his job, having developed a passion for ships and the sea as a child. He would support U.S. involvement in World War I. Part of his duties were to help plan military strategy and to tour and inspect naval bases and war zones in Europe.

In 1920, Roosevelt was surprised when he was named the vice-presidential candidate to run alongside Ohio Governor James Cox. He campaigned vigorously, but Republican Warren Harding won the election.

> **"The only limit to our realization of tomorrow will be our doubts of today."** *Franklin D. Roosevelt*

After the loss, Roosevelt moved to New York City and resumed practicing law. His political career was uncertain, especially after he contracted polio in 1921. It was three years before he could begin his political comeback. It started with a speech nominating Alfred E. Smith for president in 1924. A few years later, he would make a run for the governorship of New York and win. In his role as governor, he worked to help farmers and unemployed people as the U.S. economy began to spiral into the Great Depression.

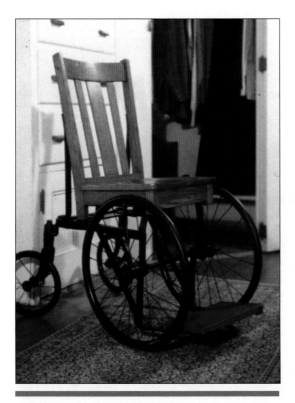

Later in life, Roosevelt would need to use a wheelchair because of polio.

POLIO

The defeat in the 1920 presidential election was not nearly as difficult for Roosevelt to overcome as was the personal struggle he soon faced. In 1921, doctors discovered he had polio, a viral disease that causes muscular atrophy and even paralysis. At age 39, Roosevelt wondered if he would ever walk again. He was fitted with braces and crutches, and after much physical exercise, he was able to walk.

Roosevelt was later told of a Georgia health resort called Warm Springs. He bathed there in warm mineral water, which helped his condition greatly. He soon bought Warm Springs and built a home on its grounds.

Roosevelt Takes Office

In 1929, the stock market crash set off the Great Depression. President Herbert Hoover's policies appeared to have little effect on improving the lives of Americans during this economic disaster. The nation began seeking a leader with new ideas.

> **"We have always held to the hope, the belief, the conviction that there is a better life, a better world, beyond the horizon."**
> *Franklin D. Roosevelt*

Roosevelt won the Democratic nomination in 1932. His platform featured public works programs, such as building roads and planting trees, to decrease unemployment. Roosevelt eagerly reminded people that Hoover had done little to solve an economic crisis that was actually getting worse. The voters agreed. Roosevelt won by more than 7 million votes.

Franklin D. Roosevelt gave his inaugural speech to the nation on March 4, 1933.

No president had ever inherited a greater economic mess than what Franklin Roosevelt faced when he took office on March 4, 1933. By then, the unemployment rate had reached a staggering 25 percent. Encampments of homeless people could be seen in every major city. Americans had lost confidence in themselves, their economic future, and their leaders. Roosevelt was not only required to reverse the direction of the American economy from the moment he became president, he had to do it in a hurry. People were suffering. Businesses were failing. Banks were closing. In his inaugural address, Roosevelt told the American people his first order of business would be putting them back to work and creating hope for the homeless.

Roosevelt wasted no time setting his plans in motion. He called for an emergency session of Congress five days after his inauguration speech. Roosevelt then called for a national "bank holiday" in which banks would close for four days. There would be no deposits, withdrawals, or loans. The federal government investigated the banks, and those that were financially sound were allowed to re-open. Meanwhile, the Federal Deposit Insurance Commission (FDIC) was created. It insured bank deposits that did not exceed $5,000. Laws were passed to prevent banks from dealing in stocks and bonds. People eventually regained their trust in the banking industry.

A mere eight days after taking office, Roosevelt began a tradition that was not only to become his trademark, but would keep the public informed and reassured throughout his time as president. His "fireside chats" were broadcast to a radio audience around the country. During these broadcasts, Roosevelt told people about his plans to help them and in turn asked for their support in convincing Congress to agree to his policies. His fireside chats attracted more listeners than most popular radio shows of the time.

> **"I pledge you—I pledge myself—to a new deal for the American people."**
> *Franklin D. Roosevelt during his 1932 campaign for president*

THE FIRST LADY

Eleanor Roosevelt would redefine the role of First Lady. No First Lady has ever played a more significant role in American society than Eleanor. As first lady, she made strong suggestions that helped her husband shape his domestic policies. Eleanor felt compassion for underprivileged Americans, especially African Americans, who were treated poorly. Following her husband's death, she was appointed as a delegate to the United Nations. She lectured and fought for racial harmony, women's rights, and world peace.

Roosevelt's New Deal

Roosevelt's presidency began on a good note. During the emergency session of Congress he had called, Roosevelt passed many reform bills. The special session of Congress was termed "The 100 Days," and Congress worked on more pieces of legislation in those 100 days than in any other period in U.S. history. The new president called all of the laws the New Deal. The New Deal was meant to help guide the United States out of the Great Depression.

One of the most important pieces of this plan was the Civilian Conservation Corps (CCC). The CCC put millions of young men back to work. They built roads, planted trees, and built dikes to prevent floods. The workers were given food and shelter, and paid $1 a day. They were expected to send most of their earnings back to their families.

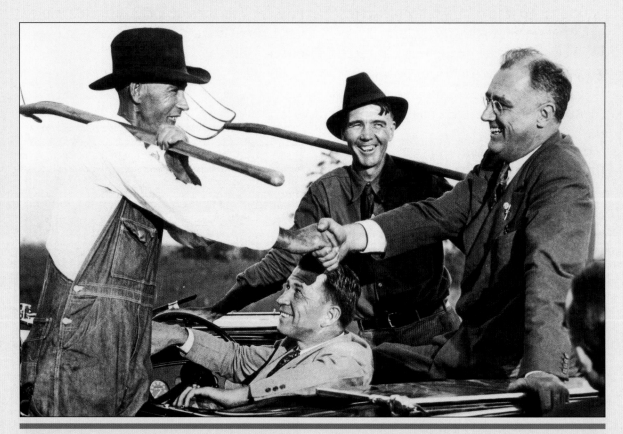

Farmers were some of the first people Roosevelt hoped to help with his New Deal programs.

Roosevelt created the Agricultural Adjustment Administration (AAA) to control the price of farm products without hurting farmers. At the time, farmers could not get a decent price for their crops. There were too many farm goods available, so food producers would not offer farmers much for their crops. The AAA prevented overproduction by paying farmers not to grow certain crops. Once there were not as many farm products available, food producers had to start paying farmers more for their crops.

Another program Roosevelt created to employ people was the Tennessee Valley Authority (TVA). The Tennessee Valley was hit hard by the Great Depression. The TVA hired people to build dams along the Tennessee River. The dams provided inexpensive electrical power to people in several states.

The National Recovery Administration (NRA) was another agency created in the first 100 days of Roosevelt's initial term in office. This wide-ranging organization guaranteed a minimum wage for employees and reduced the workweek. The NRA helped end child labor by raising the age workers needed to be. It also gave workers more freedom to organize and join **unions**. Unions fought for better working conditions and fair wages for workers.

Nobody knew for certain if such programs would dig the United States out of the Great Depression. Roosevelt's assertive approach and his confidence gave the American people hope that better days were ahead.

> "Every ounce of strength and every resource at our command we have devoted to the end of justifying your confidence."
>
> *Franklin D. Roosevelt, on his efforts to fight the Great Depression*

Political cartoonists had creative ways to show how Roosevelt's policies might help the country.

The End of Roosevelt's First Term

The initial wave of New Deal programs began showing signs of improving the economy. They decreased unemployment and increased people's confidence in the government's ability to help them, and though Roosevelt took criticism for the vast government spending behind these programs, he continued to roll out a series of new initiatives.

Roosevelt established the Securities and Exchange Commission (SEC). This organization instituted tight controls over the trading and selling of stocks. Stocks and bonds had to be registered with the SEC before they could be traded, and the SEC monitored transactions on the stock market. These controls were meant to prevent another crash, and they helped people begin reinvesting money in businesses.

In 1934, the National Housing Act was passed. This law created the Federal Housing Administration (FHA). The FHA sought to improve housing conditions and establish a system of home financing. It helped people buy houses by insuring their mortgages, or house payments, in the event that they were unable to pay.

Roosevelt continued to create works programs. The Works Progress Administration found work for a wide range of people. Roads and bridges were built. This organization found work for writers, actors, and musicians.

Women directed traffic in Alabama as part of a Works Progress Administration road program.

Roosevelt signed the Social Security Act into law, creating the modern-day social security system. This system provided retirees over the age of 65 with an income. It provided financial assistance for the unemployed and people who were disabled.

Not everyone agreed with Roosevelt's policies, however. Big businesses rallied against him for his support of organized labor. Roosevelt refused to change his course. In fact, he pushed through Congress a massive tax hike for the wealthy that provided more money for his job creation efforts.

Some of Roosevelt's policies were deemed unconstitutional. The U.S. Supreme Court struck down the Agricultural Adjustment Acts, which paid farmers not to grow crops. The courts found the National Industrial Recovery Act, which created the NRA, unconstitutional. It was allowing large companies to fix prices, which hurt small business.

These setbacks did not stop Roosevelt. A second set of Agricultural Adjustment Acts was enacted into law. They created a system in which farm surpluses were stored and then sold in times of need. The National Labor Relations Act replaced the National Industrial Recovery Act. The new law protected workers by allowing them to organize and bargain for wages and benefits using union representatives. Under this law, employers could not discriminate against union members or try to control the unions. Afterward, union membership increased. The National Labor Relations Act served to put organized labor's support solidly behind Roosevelt in future elections.

Meanwhile, all of the programs initiated early in Roosevelt's presidency continued to churn out jobs and rebuild America. Thousands of schools and hundreds of highways were being constructed, as were other public works, such as the Grand Coulee Dam in the state of Washington.

Though banking officials complained about the controls put on them by Congress, their industry had become more secure. Higher employment meant more people deposited money in banks. In turn, the banks were able to give out loans to businesses and to people who wanted to buy homes.

By the time the 1936 election rolled around in November, Roosevelt's supporters far outnumbered his critics. Though many feared massive government spending would catch up to the economy, Americans were not looking to the future. They were struggling right then and there, and Roosevelt was providing relief and hope.

> **"It is common sense to take a method and try it. If it fails, admit it frankly and try another. But above all, try something."**
>
> *Franklin D. Roosevelt, on his attempts to relieve the economic hardship of the American people*

Roosevelt's Re-election

> **"Wherever I have gone in this country I have found Americans."**
>
> *Alf Landon, in a joked-about quote during his 1936 run for president*

An incumbent president has always been difficult to defeat. Those already in office have a track record and can boast on the campaign trail about their achievements. Voters are often hesitant to mark their ballots for challengers because of a fear of the unknown, especially during times of trouble. This worked in Roosevelt's favor as he set off to convince Americans to elect him to a second term in 1936. He was able to point out that the country was in better economic shape than it had been when he took office.

There was not much Republican candidate Alf Landon could do to counter the wave of support gained by Roosevelt. The Kansas governor warned against government spending and what he claimed were Roosevelt's unconstitutional policies. Landon's attack on the New Deal severely hurt his image among voters.

Roosevelt campaigned under the slogan "We've Just Begun to Fight," which gave Americans hope that he would not rest on his early successes. They believed it showed that he understood the country was only beginning to emerge from its economic troubles. Landon hoped to attract voters by bashing Roosevelt's measures as anti-business. The unions created under Roosevelt's policies demanded higher wages and better working conditions for employees. Landon argued that unions would make it more difficult for businesses to succeed. He criticized the Social Security Act because it was

President Roosevelt talked with farmers from North Dakota on his campaign for re-election in 1936.

funded by a six percent tax increase to be shared by all employers and workers.

Roosevelt was not able to campaign as extensively as he did in 1932. His duties as president required most of his attention. His fireside chats not only served to inform Americans about the course of the country, they allowed him to plead his case to the people.

The American public would show their gratitude on election day. Roosevelt won his 1936 re-election bid by a record margin. Roosevelt won almost two-thirds of the popular vote, and he won all but eight of the 531 electoral votes. On successive election days, the American people would continue to show their support for Roosevelt. He won re-election in 1940 and would win again in 1944.

CHANGING THEIR VOTE

Up until Roosevelt's time, most African Americans had traditionally voted Republican. Republican President Abraham Lincoln led the nation through the Civil War, which resulted in the end of slavery.

During the 1936 election, the National Association for the Advancement of Colored People (NAACP) endorsed Roosevelt. This marked a shift in the African-American vote to the Democratic Party. Roosevelt's policies were seen as helping people of all races. Due to the efforts of his wife, Eleanor, several African Americans were given advisory posts with the government.

Posters were hung in support of President Roosevelt. People believed he was the right person to lead them out of the Great Depression.

World War II

The Great Depression was the dominant issue in America throughout most of the 1930s, but a war across the Atlantic Ocean soon took center stage. During this time, the Nazi Party, with Adolf Hitler as its leader, had risen to power in Germany. The German people were also known as Aryans. One of the Nazi beliefs was that the Aryan Race was superior to all other races. The Nazis persecuted people of other races, such as the Jews.

Germany formed an alliance with Italy and Japan. These three countries became known as the Axis Powers. They agreed to support each other's effort to spread their influence throughout the globe.

In the 1930s, Nazi Germany began its conquest of Europe. In 1939, it invaded Poland and soon controlled most of Western Europe. Great Britain became the lone European country standing against the German forces.

Many Americans did not fear Germany as much as Japan, which had been active militarily since the early 1930s. Japan had already begun its conquest of Asia when it invaded part of China in 1931. Roosevelt, however, saw an immediate need to help in Europe. He knew all of Western Europe would fall if Great Britain was conquered by the Nazis.

Most Americans held an **isolationist** view, believing the United States should stay neutral in the conflict, which became known as World War II. Throughout the 1940 presidential campaign, Roosevelt supported this idea. He felt he could not worry about problems overseas when there were so many economic troubles at home.

As Germany and Japan's power grew, more and more people began to believe that something had to be done to stop them. After the 1940 election, Roosevelt continued to argue that the United States should stay out of the war in Europe, but he could not remain neutral in his beliefs. In fact, he was outspoken in his view that even if the United States did not take sides militarily, it still had to support its ally, Great Britain.

LEGEND

- GERMAN REICH, ALLIES, AND OCCUPIED ZONES
- ALLIES
- AXIS CONTROLLED
- NEUTRAL

Scale 80 160 Miles

Roosevelt provided Great Britain with aid through the Lend-Lease Act, which was passed in March 1941. The law provided Great Britain and other countries that opposed the Axis Powers, such as Russia, with military aid. Not only did it thwart Germany's ambitions, but the aid helped further stimulate the U.S. economy.

ISOLATIONISM

World War I had a lasting effect on Americans despite the fact that the United States only fought in that war for one year. When war broke out again in Europe, more than half of the country believed the United States should stay out of the conflict and worry about its own problems. This view is known as isolationism.

The United States Declares War

In August 1941, Roosevelt met with British Prime Minister Winston Churchill. They agreed to the Atlantic Charter, in which the destruction of Nazi Germany was one of its primary goals. Even though Roosevelt tried to stay out of the war, this agreement drew the United States closer to the conflict in Europe.

On the morning of December 7, 1941, most people were still asleep when U.S. sailors at Pearl Harbor, Hawai'i, were suddenly awakened by the roar of Japanese planes and the blare of air raid sirens. They were being attacked, but they could not react quickly enough. Two hours later, the American Pacific fleet was in ruins. Eight battleships had been sunk. More than 180 planes were destroyed. About 3,500 Americans had been killed or wounded.

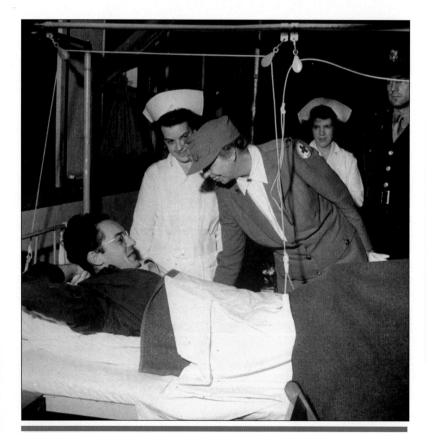

Eleanor Roosevelt visited with injured soldiers during World War II.

"Yesterday, December 7, 1941—a date which will live in infamy—the United States was suddenly and deliberately attacked by naval and air forces of the Empire of Japan."

Franklin D. Roosevelt, in requesting from Congress a declaration of war against Japan on Dec. 8, 1941

The American people were glued to their radios the next morning as Roosevelt, speaking in front of Congress, asked for a declaration of war on Japan. Congress took 33 minutes to vote in favor of it. Just three days later, Germany and Italy declared war on the United States.

Thousands of American men immediately enlisted in the U.S. military. Later, others were drafted into the service. Women were encouraged to volunteer for the first time in the nation's history, but not as soldiers. Many of them served as nurses.

The war brought change to American society. Millions of women went to work for the first time. They had to provide money and food for their families, especially with their husbands fighting thousands of miles away. They were needed to produce war materials for the massive effort.

Manufacturers throughout the country made the rapid switch from peacetime to wartime production. Roosevelt, always a champion of organized labor, took steps to ensure employees could not strike. He deemed any shutdown of businesses working toward victory in the war to be dangerous. Roosevelt made sure conflicts between businesses and workers were settled quickly to prevent strikes.

After the attack on Pearl Harbor, Franklin D. Roosevelt signed a declaration of war on Japan.

INTERNMENT CAMPS

After the declaration of war against Japan, the U.S. government forced many Japanese Americans, most of whom lived on the west coast, to relocate to internment camps. These camps were large detention centers. Nearly 70 percent of the Japanese-Americans in these camps were born in the United States. More than 110,000 people had been sent to internment camps by the end of 1942.

Roosevelt's Legacy

"His role in insuring the downfall of Adolf Hitler is alone enough to earn him a respected place in history."

Robert Divine, writer, on the legacy of Franklin D. Roosevelt

With U.S. assistance, the Allies began turning the tide in Europe. Not only were they able to launch an invasion of Europe in 1944, but by that time, Germany had been pushed out of the Soviet Union. Nazi forces were on the retreat. In April 1945, Hitler took his own life, and Germany surrendered. The war with Japan was also nearing an end. In May, the United States dropped two atomic bombs on Japan, forcing it to surrender. By time the war was over, 50 million people had died.

Roosevelt, however, would not see the end of the war. Weeks before Hitler's death, Roosevelt's doctor ordered him to rest at his home in Warm Springs. On April 12, Roosevelt began complaining about a terrible headache. He had suffered a cerebral hemorrhage when a blood vessel broke in his brain. Roosevelt died a few hours later. He was 63 years old. His vice president, Harry S. Truman, would lead the Allies to their final victory in World War II.

A medal was created to honor Franklin D. Roosevelt for helping the country through its worst economic troubles.

When Roosevelt died, he had been the longest-serving president in U.S. history. No president before him had served more than two terms, and Roosevelt had been elected to four. In 1951, the 22nd Amendment would be enacted into law, limiting presidents to two terms in office.

Roosevelt will forever be remembered as one of the greatest leaders in American history because of his confidence, his ability to sway voters and decision-makers, and his strong morals and values. Roosevelt was a champion of the American people and led the nation forward during its greatest economic struggle. He empowered workers by improving working conditions, shortening workweeks, and making it easier for them to organize unions. He gave the poor and homeless hope when they had lost everything. He took a nation on the brink of economic collapse and set it back on the path to prosperity.

Some might think that coming from a wealthy family made it easy for Roosevelt. Rather than living off his family's money, he worked his entire professional life to improve the lives of the American people.

A statue of Franklin D. Roosevelt stands in Grosvenor Square, London, honoring the support he gave to Great Britain during World War II.

Thousands of mourners showed their feelings during Franklin D. Roosevelt's funeral procession.

Timeline

The era began with great promise and ended with great promise. The time in between, however, was dominated by economic hardship and war. Hoover took office as troubles in the United States began. Some people felt he failed the country during its darkest hours, but Hoover will always be known as a great humanitarian for his efforts to help people in need.

1920-1925	1926-1930	1931-1935
PRESIDENTS		
Hoover is appointed secretary of commerce by President Woodrow Wilson in 1921. 	Herbert Hoover is elected to be the 31st president of the United States in 1928.	In 1932, Franklin D. Roosevelt is elected to be the 32nd president of the United States.
UNITED STATES		
In 1924, Congress votes to pay World War I veterans a bonus for their service during the war.	The stock market crashes in 1929, marking the beginning of the Great Depression.	Because of Hoover's unpopularity, the "Hoover Dam" is renamed the "Boulder Dam" by Roosevelt in 1935. It is later changed back to Hoover Dam.
WORLD		
In 1922, several countries with influence in the Pacific Ocean sign the Nine-Power Treaty, which recognizes China as an independent country.	The stock market crash in the United States in 1929 marks the beginning of worldwide economic troubles.	Hitler's Nazi Party takes control of Germany in 1933. 

When Roosevelt took office, he made immediate changes to governmental policies. His New Deal turned the economy around as another tragic event loomed. Not only did Roosevelt deal with the Great Depression during his presidency, he also led the United States through the destruction of World War II. Through Roosevelt's determination, the country had a bright future.

1936-1939	1940-1944	1945
PRESIDENTS		
Roosevelt is elected to a second term in office in 1936. 	In 1940, Roosevelt is elected to a third term in office.	Roosevelt dies in 1945, and Harry S. Truman becomes president.
UNITED STATES		
While war is brewing overseas, Americans take an isolationist view and oppose U.S. involvement in the crisis.	Japan's attack on Pearl Harbor draws the United States into World War II in 1941.	The United States ends the war against Japan by dropping two atomic bombs on the country in 1945.
WORLD		
In 1939, Nazi Germany invades Poland, marking the beginning of World War II. 	U.S. troops lead an invasion of Nazi-controlled Europe.	Germany surrenders after Hitler's death in 1945, ending World War II in Europe.

Activity

After the German invasion of Poland launched World War II, most Americans took an isolationist point of view and believed the United States should stay neutral. Others felt that the nation needed to join the fray. From September 1939 to December 1941, Congress debated the role the United States would play in the war in Europe.

Decide for yourself whether the United States should take an isolationist stance or be more involved in world affairs.

First, look at World War II. In one column, write down the reasons the United States should have stayed out of World War II, and in a second column, write why it should have fought in the war. Do not think about the outcome of the war, but what things were like before the United States entered the war.

Next, looking at your list, decide for yourself what the United States should have done. Think about how things might have been different had the United States entered the war earlier and what the benefits were to staying out of the war as long as it did.

After you make your decision about World War II, do this activity for other world events. The United States has been involved in the Revolutionary War, the Civil War, the Vietnam War, the Korean War, the Persian Gulf War, and the Iraq War. Make a list of reasons to be involved in these conflicts and reasons to be an isolationist. Compare the lists, and decide what your course of action would be if you were president.

Quiz

1. Herbert Hoover grew up on a small farm in Iowa, but eventually became a wealthy business owner. What did he do?
   A. Struck it rich in a gold mine
   B. Became a professional boxer in China
   C. Started up an engineering company

2. What did Franklin D. Roosevelt call his Sunday radio speeches to the American public?
   A. Today's Talk
   B. Words from the White House
   C. Fireside Chats

3. Franklin D. Roosevelt was related in what way to former president Theodore Roosevelt?
   A. Cousins
   B. Brothers
   C. Father and son

4. True or False? Franklin D. Roosevelt was the longest serving president in U.S. history.

5. Franklin D. Roosevelt started many programs during the Great Depression to create jobs. What did he call his approach?
   A. The New Deal
   B. A Hopeful Start
   C. The Great Plan

6. True or False? World War II began when Japan bombed Pearl Harbor.

7. True or False? Franklin D. Roosevelt is called the Great Humanitarian.

8. What event set off the Great Depression?
   A. Unemployment
   B. Stock market crash
   C. World War I

9. True or False? Herbert Hoover lost in his bid for re-election in 1936.

Answers 1. C 2. C 3. A 4. True 5. A 6. False. The war began when Germany invaded Poland. The United States entered the war after the attack on Pearl Harbor. 7. False. Herbert Hoover earned this nickname for helping people during World War I. 8. B 9. True

Further Research

Books

To find out more about United States presidents, visit your local library. Most libraries have computers that connect to a database for researching information. If you input a key word, you will be provided with a list of books in the library that contain information on that topic. Non-fiction books are arranged numerically, using their call number. Fiction books are organized alphabetically by the author's last name.

Websites

The World Wide Web is a good source of information. Reputable websites include government sites, educational sites, and online encyclopedias. Visit the following sites to learn more about U.S. presidents.

The official White House website offers a short history of the U.S. presidency, along with biographical sketches and portraits of all the presidents to date. **www.whitehouse.gov/history/presidents**

This website contains background information, election results, cabinet members, and notable events for each of the presidents. **www.ipl.org/div/potus**

Explore the lives and careers of every U.S. president on the PBS website. **www.pbs.org/wgbh/amex/presidents**

Glossary

Allies: the United States, Russia, Great Britain, and any other countries that fought against the Axis Powers during World War II

Axis Powers: the nations of Germany, Japan, and Italy, which fought on the same side during World War II

campaigns: competitions by rival political candidates leading up to an election

Congress: the legislative body of the U.S. government, consisting of the Senate and House of Representatives; Congress enacts laws

depression: a period of severe and lengthy economic hardship

isolationist: a person who believes that a nation should focus on issues within its own country instead of getting involved in world affairs, such as wars

Nazi: the political party, led by Adolf Hitler, that took control of Germany

nominee: a politician who a party names to run for office

stock market: where people trade stocks and bonds

unions: organizations of workers that negotiate with employers with a goal to maximize wages and improve working conditions

veterans: people who have served in the military

Index